The
Letter

A Memoir

CHRISTINE
MERSER

The Letter
First Edition

Copyright © 2025 by Christine Merser

ISBN: 979-8-9922189-2-3 (Print)
ISBN: 979-8-9922189-3-0 (Kindle)
ISBN: 979-8-9922189-6-1 (ePub)

Library of Congress Control Number: 2025903666

Published by Apricity Publishing
Wiscasset, Maine
ApricityPublishing.com

Printed in the United States

DEDICATION

For My Mother

Whose one mistake took so much from the rest of her life. I see you on the moon every month, Mom, and send you the love you have always deserved.

CONTENTS

PART
One

DAY ONE

I'm walking down dim, empty hallways that seem to go on forever. I finally arrive at the ICU. I find the room. I think it's already past ten o'clock.

She's tied to the bed, my mother, so she can't pull the tubes out of her nose. She tosses fitfully as I enter. Her mountainous stomach rises in perfect unison with her breathing, and I'm surprised that her fat doesn't sink into her when she lies on her back the way mine does.

A private nurse sits at the end of her bed, sort of staring into space.

"Is she asleep?" I ask.

"I don't think so. The nurse was just talking to her. You can speak to her if you want."

As I walk to the bed, I wonder just what I can possibly say to my mother, who, not twenty-four hours ago, swallowed two bottles of pills, alone in her own guest bathroom, in the middle of the night. I feel the shame of witnessing something deeply private, as if I'd walked in on a moment not meant for anyone else.

"Mom, hi. It's me, Anne."

She opens her eyes, turns her head to me, sort of feeling around as best she can with the restraints on her arms, so I take the plunge and take her hand. Holding her hand is difficult. I can't help but look down and wonder if, at any time in my life, I held this hand thinking she would show me the way somewhere.

"Hi."

"Mom, I came because I wanted to tell you that I love you, and I'm sorry you felt you needed to do this to yourself."

"Well, I fucked this up, just like the rest of my life."

She starts to cry. Little tears that sort of fill up her eyes and spill over one at a time at the corners.

"Maybe you need help, Mom. And now, maybe, we'll get it for you."

She lets go of my hand.

"Where's your husband?"

My husband?

"He's at home with Ali, Mom. I came with Lisa."

"What time is it?"

"It's just after ten o'clock. Can I get you anything?"

"Ten o'clock in the morning?"

"No, Mom, ten o'clock at night. I was out all day and Harvey just reached me. You've been here since morning."

"How's your family?"

My family? You are my family, Mom, so how are you?

"Fine, Mom. Everybody's fine."

"Where's Eva?"

My older sister, Eva, lives about two hours away and having agreed with our stepfather, Harvey, that maybe Mom didn't really do this on purpose, decided it was best to find out what the situation was before she made the lengthy trip. I take a second to think about how this decision is so central to the way my family functions and am struck by the absurdity of it all.

"Eva's at home, Mom. She wanted to know if you'd like her to come."

"If she wants to."

"I think she would like to do whatever you would like her to."

Mom makes the face. I wouldn't call it a real scowl. It's the face she uses when she wants to tell me I shouldn't press her. Let's face it, you shouldn't have to say you want the kids to come. Wouldn't the act alone summon them?

"I'll call her when I get home. She'll be here tomorrow. I wish there was something I could say, Mom."

"I'm thirsty."

I turn to the nurse and realize she is staring at me.

"Can she have water?"

"No, not with the tubes."

"You can't have water, Mom. Tomorrow when they take the tubes out. It's time for me to go now. I'll come back to-morrow."

"Okay."

"I love you, Mom."

Those tears start again.

"I love you, too."

As I leave the hospital, I have to remind myself that I didn't do this. I remind myself that my mother is a woman who is a product of her own past, not mine. I remind myself that this is not my fault.

My letter, oh my God! My letter. I mailed it Monday. Had it arrived? Oh hell, how could she choose yesterday to do this?

I try to focus on what we need to do. But instead, the words of my little sister to my older sister last summer start echoing in my tired head.

"Please tell Anne to stop trying to kill our mother."

* * *

It's raining as we head back to the city, and my friend, Lisa, who drove out with me, is listening intently as I describe my visit. Her mother had been institutionalized numerous times for doing just what my mom did. A new bond makes the intimacy stifling.

The car phone rings, and I know it's my shrink, Simon Levy. Some sort of sick excitement takes hold. After all, I had predicted this. When he would ask me what is the worst thing that could happen if I confronted my mother in a letter, I would always immediately answer, "She will die."

I pick up the phone and it is Levy. He sounds shaken, and I sense he has spoken to my husband. I start to cry. Lisa tells me to pull over so she can drive. I tell Levy to hold on while we switch places.

"Is she going to live?"

God, I never asked. Of course she is. She was speaking to me.

"I guess so. She spoke to me."

"How are you?"

The sobs take over. Really big ones. The kind that shake your body and make you gasp for air.

We talk for a while and he tries to tell me that the anger, fear, and pain that I'm feeling are fine. Just fine. I want to shout that feeling like this is not fine. No one should ever feel like this.

We arrange to speak the next day, and in the meantime, he will make some calls about getting her into Columbia Presbyterian Hospital. Supposedly it's one of the best places for this type of thing. Just what type of thing is this?

DAY TWO

My husband, David, and I arrive at the hospital in the late morning. He had a tennis game earlier and didn't want to disappoint the other three players. It's still raining slightly and as we go through the circular drive, I see the back of my sister, Eva, walking up the sidewalk, ever so slowly, no umbrella, arms at her side.

Swinging limply, in her left hand, held by one leg, is a white stuffed animal and a plastic bag that looks as if it came from the drug store. I pull the car over, get out, leaving David to park. We hug before saying anything.

"How are you?" I ask.

"Fine. I saw her and went out to get some stuff I thought she might like."

My sister hands me the stuffed animal and shows me the gifts she purchased for Mom. We're not a stuffed animal kind of family but who knows what Eva is thinking. I look at the items she pulls out of the bag and think how it will ensure that we won't have to have any real conversations. A full five minutes can be filled with the giving of trinkets. Five minutes is all you're allowed in the ICU.

"I got her this Evian freshen-up spray so she can feel better. See?"

She sprays a mist on my face and all I can think of is how aerosol cans are bad for the environment. So is suicide.

"I always feel better if I feel fresh, and she probably hasn't had a bath since ..."

"Since Thursday," I finish for her. "Did you see Harvey?"

"Yeah, I ran into him as he was leaving. He looks so lost."

"Did Mom say anything?"

"I asked her if she was glad it didn't work and she said yes."

"You asked her that?"

"Uh huh. I also asked her if she planned it or if it was spur-of-the-moment."

"You are so brave. What did she say?"

"She said it was spur-of-the-moment."

I wonder if Eva believes it.

We walk for a moment in silence. When we're just outside the door to her room, I look over at Eva, who raises her eyebrows. I smile at her and as we walk into the room, we both head to the same side of the bed. It seems to me she holds back just a second, as if she's hoping I will walk to the position closest to our mother. So that's what I do.

"Hi, Mom."

"Hi. You were here last night. Were you wearing a blue coat?"

"Yes. That was me." She seems thrilled that she could recognize the coat.

"How is Ali?"

How is Ali? How would I know? She's been farmed out for the duration.

"Fine. She's just fine."

"What did you tell her?"

"I told her that you had taken some medicine that made you very sick because you didn't take it properly. That you were in the hospital, and that you would be okay."

"Oh."

Is it possible that I detect a note of disappointment?

Nurse No Nonsense walks in at this point waving the written instructions about visiting hours being on the hour, two people, for five minutes.

My sister and I leave and head to the waiting room.

"So, what else did Mom say?" I ask when we sit down.

"She said she wants a Christian doctor."

"What?"

"I knew you would say that. She's entitled to ask for what she wants."

We had already discussed that Mom would have to be moved to one of the institutions in the city for inpatient care, and we had planned on figuring that out with Stepfather Harvey later in the day. I was already set on what my Jewish shrink had suggested, Columbia Presbyterian, and had mentioned this to Eva who seemed to agree.

"Eva, that is ridiculous. There are no Christian shrinks in New York. At least not any good ones. And might I point out that my child is Jewish, so what is she trying to say?"

"Don't tell David."

Ah, how my family loves secrets. At this most opportune moment, the elevator doors open, and out steps David with *The New York Times* under his arm.

"Hi. Mom wants a Christian shrink."

"There are no good Christian shrinks."

I look pointedly at Eva to show her that I don't keep secrets. We all sit in silence waiting for twelve o'clock; David reading his paper, Eva picking at her chewed-off fingernails, and me sitting here wondering why there is nothing any of us has to say. It occurs to me that my husband hasn't asked how my mother is. Harvey gets off the elevator.

Harvey is fat. He's the kind of fat that changes the way he walks. He leans back, leading with his oversized belly and following with the rest of him. His jowls sag sort of like those gross dogs that are all skin. But the worst thing about him is that his lips are always wet. If he kisses you, you have to wipe off your face.

"How are you, Harvey?" David asks.

"I'm okay. I just don't know why she would do this. We went away for our anniversary last weekend and we had a wonderful time."

Just how wonderful could it have been Harvey?

"In fact, she told me that if I died, she didn't think she'd ever remarry. I don't understand what happened."

As he rambles on, I listen to the self-centered nature of his conversation. Of course she wouldn't remarry.

Finally, Dr. Donovan arrives. Dr. Donovan has been my mother's doctor for the last eight years or so, since she broke her leg falling down the stairs at her needlepoint shop. My first husband's name was Donovan but for whatever reason, my mother used to insist on introducing me as Anne Dunovan, instead of Donovan. Somehow, she always seems to pronounce the doctor's name correctly, though. It used to make me angry. Now I just feel sad.

"I've just spoken with Barbara and let's discuss now what comes next. First, can we introduce ourselves?"

We all go around introducing ourselves in our most mature manner and then he continues.

"Your mother and I are not just doctor and patient. We are close friends. I have trusted her and still do. If she told me this was all a mistake and wanted to leave here tomorrow, I would believe her and let her go."

Swell.

He continues, "But your mother isn't saying that. She says she just didn't want to wake up anymore, and she is sorry it didn't work. We must all decide what to do for her now. This hospital is a fine place, although I am sure all you people from the city think we are hicks. But your mother is a public figure, and therefore we owe it to her to keep this as quiet as possible. She needs to decide who she wants to share this with, so going to the city may be the best idea."

My mom has been the mayor of Westport, Connecticut for the last eight years. She did not run in the last election and has been asked to make a bid for Congress by the Republican Committee in Connecticut. It strikes me that my mother didn't seem to want that or she wouldn't have done what she did.

"Excuse me, but before we discuss that, could you please explain to us what my mom took and what her physical condition is?" I ask.

"Oh yes. Of course. Forgive me. I am a bit shaken by all this. Your mother took Ativan, a mild sedative. I think she took more than a hundred pills but we are not sure. Harvey, you found two empty containers in the trash, is that right?"

Harvey is thrilled to be the empty container expert.

"Yes, Doctor, there were two empty containers in the trash, and my neighbor who I called over, looked it up in her pharmaceutical book and said we should get her to the hospital right away."

You mean when you found her you didn't dial 911? You called the neighbor? Why? Why waste all that time?

"Thanks, Harvey. Now there is a problem in that the tests that were run say Barbara had nothing in her, but anyone who saw her here knows she was a mess. There must have been an error or slip-up here at the lab. We are rerunning the tests this afternoon."

What the hell is this? Why wait to rerun the tests until this afternoon, more than twenty-four hours later?

"Does anyone feel strongly about where Barbara should go?"

Thank God for David, the renowned investment banker, who now steps in and does his Merger and Acquisitions number on us all, getting everyone to agree to Levy's suggestion of Columbia Presbyterian Hospital. Harvey, of course, is concerned about the connection to me and voices it with so much anger that I am pleased that I am causing him so much anxiety. I am also surprised he shows his dislike of me, which in better times he hides. His comments are usually when no one else is around, and I realize he is close to the edge.

The rest of the day is a blur of arrangements, polite conversations, stress. The camaraderie that my sister and I shared in the early hours is replaced by the roles reinforced over the thirty-eight years of being siblings. Eva, the sensitive, pained one stepping back so Anne, the take charge, get-it-done one can take responsibility, make the arrangements, and feel as if action will solve the problem.

The day is so long that when, at last, David and I arrive home, I go back to my office, sit at my computer and wonder how it's possible that in twenty-four short hours everything that has been my family for thirty-eight years is no longer.

DAY FIVE

I arrive at Levy's office filled with that unexplained excitement again. I realize that my fears of her not being able to handle my letter, or my trying to change what has been the dynamic between us all these years, was not without truth. And, somehow, that makes me feel a bit better about all the self-doubt I've had, most likely all my life.

All of that fades as I walk in the door and the tears begin again.

"Hi Anne, how are you?"

"I'm tired."

"Did your mother check in at Columbia yesterday?"

"Yes, thanks for everything you did. She's there, although it wasn't easy."

"After speaking to your stepfather on Saturday, I'm sure you are right."

"So, you got to talk to Harvey. I guess you got a dose of what it's like."

"Well, he surprised even me. I was struck the entire time I was on the phone with him, that he was trying to be on his best behavior, and yet, his hatred of you was in every word as well as in his tone of voice. He seemed less concerned with where your mother would be going, and more concerned that you have no say in anything."

Why do I feel happy with that? Confirmation of what I have always known and others denied?

"Your mother's doctor said a few things that struck me. The first was that your mother's persona in the community is one of the fat, jolly person."

The fat jolly person? My God, my worst nightmare! I have to struggle to pay attention as he continues.

"He said that he felt this was a serious attempt because she is so embedded in that role that he was surprised she would risk losing it even after death."

Afraid to lose her persona, that persona, after death? God.

My sisters and I were brought up to behave with the outsider in mind. Always. The commitment to serving the outside world instead of yourself and your own family is a lifelong one. It never occurred to me, however, that the commitment extended to the afterlife as well.

My shoulders feel heavy with the burden of this new realization. I think about going home and making sure that my drawers are in order. That anything that I don't want everyone in the world to see must be destroyed, just in case.

"Did he say anything else?"

"Yes, he said that your mother told him she hated Harvey and that after having gone away with him the weekend before to celebrate their sixteenth anniversary, she couldn't bear the thought of continuing."

DAY SEVEN

Eva arrives at six o'clock on the dot to ride together to the hospital to visit with our mother. I meet her in my building's lobby laden with a large basket of flowers, a paper bag filled with some things that Mom has asked me to bring, including note paper, envelopes, and stamps. I've never received a letter from my mother. Maybe my mother has a whole other life that I know nothing about. A world in which she writes letters and personal notes?

"Hi, Eva. How's it going?"

She's hostile. Angry.

"Great. It's going great. I'm sitting here waiting for you so we can ride up with your driver to see our mother in the psych ward. So far, it's going great."

"Well, I'm feeling okay. I'm actually looking forward to seeing her."

We get in the car and I turn and face her as our driver, Victor, speeds toward the hospital. My God, her face is all puffy and she is sort of slumped over. She looks so fragile, which over the years I've come to realize is her perfect ruse. She glances over at me, aware that I'm staring, makes a funny face and takes my hand. It startles me. I think that this is the second time in a week that I'm holding hands with someone in my family, and that in the thirty-eight years prior to this, I have no memory of touching my family, except the perfunctory hello peck on the cheek.

"So, what did your shrink say?" Eva asks.

"He said that this isn't the time to confront her with the fact that I'm pissed off big time about what she did. He said that if I try and do my routine of beating her into seeing it my way, she will not hear me. I think that I'm going to tell her again how sorry I am that she chose to do this."

"Hmm."

We finally arrive and walk into the hospital. There is only one floor for psychiatric inpatients, and the other floors have something to do with eyes. When the receptionist hears us say which floor we want, she looks up at us in an openly curious way. I want to tell her that I'm not my mother.

We arrive on the floor and ring a bell to be let in. The large ring of keys that the nurse is carrying reminds me of *One Flew Over the Cuckoo's Nest*. Once we enter, though, it feels as if we are in a dormitory lounge area; everyone sitting around talking as if they are heading to class in a few minutes.

I try not to stare at the people. I wonder if anyone else has to try this hard to not stare at the patients and wonder what they are doing in this place. What their stories are. I imagine it must be the first thing they ask each other. "So, what are you in for?"

We sit in my mother's room talking about less than nothing for what seems to me to be a long, long time. Eva is pacing, extolling the virtues of the book she has brought my mother. My sister, the author of three books about such things as selling Girl Scout cookies and being a grown up, always turns librarian and grammatical expert when she is nervous.

I used to wonder, when she would correct me, if my grammar deteriorated in these family situations or if she just noticed it more when she was anxious. Seven years of therapy have taught me that perhaps, just perhaps, mind you, my grammar is fine and she isn't.

I can't agree with her recommendation this time, however. She has brought William Styron's book, *Darkness Visible*, on his experience of being hospitalized for depression. Although she claims to have read it, I don't believe her because anyone who read it would not bring it to someone who has just attempted suicide. I, who did read it, pretend I haven't and stare out the window. And so continues the patterns of my family.

I feel myself sinking into my own depression. I had so wanted to visit my mother and have a real conversation about what happened. Find some way to connect and ease her pain and my own. They must be connected in some way. I just don't know how. Why am I always so vulnerable to these things; arriving for every event with my mother, even this one, filled with what always turns out to be unfulfilled expectations? I decide that I will not go away this time without trying.

"Mom," I interrupt. "I want to say something." My breathing is short and it takes three gulps of air to get out as many words. "I want you to know how sorry I am that you felt you needed to do this. I can't imagine feeling that low, but it must be awful. When I think about you and last Thursday night, I am so sorry that none of us could have helped you find another way."

There. It's done. I look up from the window to her bed, and she is still alive, sitting cross-legged, looking at me with tears welling.

"Thank you, Anne. I do feel awful. I want to talk with you girls about it, but not now; when we're all together. Until then, I think I don't want to talk about it."

You girls. Why do I hate the plural you?

"No problem, Mom. I just didn't want the visit to go by without saying it."

"Thank you."

I look over at Eva, certain that she will be glaring in disapproval. Instead, she looks as if she missed the plot. Time to go.

"Well, I guess we better go."

"Great. I'm so glad you girls came."

On the way out, waiting for the nurse to come open the door, I look at the bulletin board and notice a sign-up sheet for a brunch the floor is having on Saturday. There, about the sixth name down, is my mom's name, written in the left-handed script I have known as my mother's my whole life. Barbara. She is going to go and be a part of this group. Across from her name in big, childlike letters is the name Chef Benedetto.

"Who's that, Mom?"

"That's Ben. He's the one over there."

She points to the table at the right of the elevator where ten or so patients are seated, talking and laughing as if they were at a café in Paris, discussing America's latest scandal.

"He's here for drugs."

Her voice is that of a conspirator. Almost as if she was the head of the floor. It's the closest she's been to us mentally the entire visit, and it terrifies me. It's almost as if she's with her tribe now.

"Oh. Here's the nurse now, girls, better run. Good-bye."

As the door shuts and locks loudly behind us, I glance through the small window of the door thinking that our mother might be looking out at us, or slowly heading back to her room, probably to think about the rest of her life.

In fact, without hesitation, she immediately turns away from the door marking her "girls" leaving, and heads eagerly toward the table to join the ten other patients.

DAY EIGHT

I'm lying in bed. It's almost midnight, and my younger sister, Lauren, is back from the Caribbean Island she was basking on when this happened.

"Anne, Harvey has your letter."

"What?"

"He has the letter. Are you deaf? He says he found it, unopened, but if you hold it up to the light, you can see some of the words through the envelope. He said that he checked to see if she had steamed it open and resealed it, but he didn't think so."

"What did you say to him, Lauren?"

Lauren is known for telling you what you want to hear, not to be confused with telling you what someone actually said. She is also notorious for repeating everything you didn't say to the other side. One is always careful when speaking to her.

"I told him if he had an ounce of class, he would send it back to you unopened."

Well, that clinches it. I won't see that letter again during my lifetime. It's been more than a week since the event, and the letter has trailed around after me everywhere I've gone.

In an effort to assist with whatever they are planning to do, I had told Harvey about it and asked if he found it opened anywhere in her things. He convincingly told me he hadn't seen it. I wonder if he thinks that Lauren won't tell me that he has it.

"Hmm."

"I've had a million calls about the letter, you know," Lauren adds.

"Really, who?"

She starts down the list: Linda (Mom's best friend), Jenna (our cousin), Aunt Sharon (Mom's sister), and Connie (Mom's friend).

"I don't know, a lot," she says.

"What do they want to know?"

"What the letter said. Harvey told everyone it's why Mom took the pills."

I can only sit in silence, the pain becoming stifling. There's not enough air in the room.

"Why don't they call and ask me directly?"

"They don't feel close enough."

"So they ask you?"

"Anyway, Harvey wants me to meet him tomorrow."

"What for?"

"I think he wants to talk about money. He doesn't have any, and they had no insurance."

"What? Are you fucking kidding me?"

"Are you going deaf again? They had no insurance. It lapsed the day before she did it. He didn't pay the bill. And she's already built up a bill of $30,000."

"Jesus. Don't tell me. You're supposed to ask me for the money. Right?"

"I don't know. I'll tell you after I speak to him tomorrow."

"Lauren, I've got to go."

"I'll call you as soon as I've talked to him."

"Great. Whatever."

She didn't open the letter. Relief. A monsoon of it. The desire to call everyone in the world and tell them is squelched by the knowledge that it doesn't matter. People believe whatever absolves them of responsibility. I suppose it would help if I told them what was in it, but I can't. The letter was to my mother, not to them. I stand cemented in the desire to maintain my own privacy.

What I really want is to sleep without my fists clenching.

DAY THIRTY-TWO

I'm asleep and hear in the distance a phone ringing. I realize it's the middle of the night. I bolt upright, my heart pounding and reach for the phone.

"Hello?!"

"Hello, is John there?"

"John? I'm sorry you have the wrong number."

"I'm sorry."

Click.

I hang up the phone, look out the window at the sleeping city and try to feel calm. Even in my deep, predawn sleep, I'm alert to what seems will be the inevitable. That the next time she tries, she might be successful.

I wonder if I was dreaming about it. I count off the weeks: one, two, three, four, five. It seems like years, or is it minutes? I realize that from this moment on, I will measure time in a new way. Before Mom tried to die. After Mom tried to die. Like a crack in the timeline of my life, dividing everything into what came before and what's left now.

DAY THIRTY-SIX

I sit looking at the phone wondering how much longer I can avoid making the call to ask my mother how things are going. She's been out of the hospital almost a week, and I'm trying to show I'm interested, but not hovering. She was safe at the hospital.

It's been three days since I've checked on her, and I sit wondering if she's at home. Where would she go? Lunch with friends? I pick up the phone and dial.

"Hi, Mom. It's me."

"Hi me. I was just thinking about giving you a call."

"What a coincidence. How are you?"

"Fine, how are you?"

So, we're back to that. I want to tell her that she no longer has the right to answer my question in the old way. She lost the right to her privacy, to saying nothing about how she's feeling when she did what she did. She went public with how she was feeling, and there's no backing out now. You can say that you don't want to say how you feel. You can say you feel like shit. You can say you are glad to see the sun. You cannot say, fine, and how are you.

"I'm fine, Mom. I was thinking about you and wondering how it feels to be home."

"It feels nice. I will be coming to the city twice a week for my sessions with Dr. Clark, which will be difficult. It's a real trek, and I wish there was someone out here that I could speak with."

"Have you told him you feel that way?"

"No, but I will. I'm not ready yet."

Not ready yet. Talk about repetition. Eva told me that Mom said she wasn't ready yet to discuss what happened with us. Lauren told me that Mom wasn't ready yet to call some of the people who had spent the last weeks worrying about her. Now, she's not ready to tell her shrink that it isn't working with him for some ridiculous reason. As if a forty-minute ride into the city is a real barrier.

"How is the therapy going, Mom? Do you think you're getting anywhere?"

"Well, yes, that's what I wanted to call you about. I want to get you girls together to talk about this, but I spent yesterday discussing with him whether what happened to me is hereditary. That's my big concern now. That this not affect you girls."

"What?!"

"Well, I wanted to be sure that the odds were not increased for you and your sisters because of what happened to me."

I long to say, "What happened to you didn't *happen* to you. You are a part of it." I long to say, "Perhaps you haven't noticed, but I have not handled my life thus far the way you've handled yours, so don't worry. I won't take pills in the dead of night. Not ever." I long to say, "Don't you ever compare me to you again. Ever. Do you hear me? Never."

Mostly, I long to say, "Mom, please don't hide behind your imagined motherhood."

"So, what did he say?"

"I was relieved to have him say that the odds don't increase much for you girls."

Much. Such a key word for four innocuous letters. I wonder why he is letting her avoid her stuff by focusing on us.

"I can't imagine, in my worst nightmare, where you were that night. You must have been in a lot of pain."

"Actually, Anne, one of the things that was surprising was how easy it was."

"What do you mean?"

"When I was standing at the sink, swallowing the pills, I was surprised at how easy it was. I always thought it would be hard, but it wasn't."

My stomach turns with the image.

"Okay, Mom. So, it was easy by the time you got to swallowing the pills. But what got you there? What was it, Mom? What made you feel so badly?"

"For years now, I have awakened each morning with a feeling of dread. I have had violent thoughts in my head a lot. I was happy to think that I wouldn't have them anymore."

Violent thoughts? About whom? What? There is an edge to her voice that feels threatening. I am not frightened, though. Let her try. She can't kill me with this stuff. I've come too far for her to do any more damage than she already has.

I am in the seventh grade. I come downstairs and my mother says something. I don't answer her, and I start to cry. My father comes in yelling at her, asking her what she did to me to make me cry. She throws the spoon at him and starts screaming that she is sick and tired of the way he treats her. Standing there watching her, it's clear to me, that the truth is, she hates me because he likes me better than her.

"What about you, Anne? How do you feel?"

"I was terrified, Mom. Had you gotten my letter?" There, the first word about it is out. I wonder if she's been told about it and hasn't mentioned it, which would be true to form. Why let me off the hook? "I thought you must have because Harvey said it wasn't there, but then he told Lauren and Joseph that he had the letter. He wasn't going to do anything with it until he was ready. Has he given it to you?"

"No."

No. That's it? No? So, someone has told you about it. Or maybe you saw it and didn't bother to open it. You aren't going to say anything about it? Just let everyone think it was my fault, and never tell your husband that he has no right to keep your child's mail from you? Or to blame something on your child that you told the doctors was about him? No Sophie's choice in my history.

I'm in college. My aunt is yelling at me that it hurt my mother to death that when I lived in St. Maarten with my father for a year before going to college, I never once wrote her or called to let her know I was okay.

I am stunned by her assault. I tell her that I did write. I did call. She says my mother is a lovely person and would never lie. I ask my mother and she says she doesn't remember the phone calls, and she never got a letter.

Ten years later, looking through mementos at her house one wintry day, I come across the letters tied in a bundle. Opened. Doesn't a killer usually get rid of the evidence? I hold them up and ask her why she lied. She says she has no idea what I'm talking about.

The silence continues until I break it.

"I hope that things are getting better for you, Mom."

"They are. I'll speak to you next week."

"Bye, Mom."

"Bye, Anne."

DAY FORTY-FOUR

I sit by the ocean at our country house, looking through my sister's wedding pictures from last September. I'm picking out my mother in all the shots. She looks dead. No smile. No frown. Nothing. I wonder how I could have missed it. I don't remember her being there. I realize these could have been the last pictures I had of her alive.

I think about how ugly her dress is.

DAY FIFTY-SEVEN

I have just hung up the phone and decide to turn the page of my wall calendar. There staring me in the face is May, and Mother's Day.

How the hell can we address that day with her? What could we possibly say? What is there left to celebrate, or to pretend to celebrate?

I decide to give both my sisters a call and see if they want to do something together.

"Hi Lauren, it's me. Mother's Day is next Sunday."

"Yeah, I know. What do you want to do?"

"Nothing. So, what *should* we do?"

She laughs. Lauren loves to laugh. It's nice.

"Do you want to go to Pelham Country Club?" she asks.

"Yeah. Sure. Sounds good."

"Should we do lunch or dinner?"

"Lunch. Let's definitely do lunch. Much, much better than dinner. Will you call her?"

"Yes."

"Okay, call me and tell me what she says."

"Okay. Bye."

"I'll call Eva. Bye."

As I look down at Central Park from twenty-four flights up, I remember that Mother's Day is for me too.

DAY SIXTY

We are sitting in Dr. Levy's office, my mother and me. It's our second joint session and the letter hangs out there waiting to be discussed.

"Barbara, Anne told me that Harvey has her letter."

"Yes."

"Have you asked him for it?"

"No."

"Do you have any desire to have it or to read it?"

"No."

"Oh, well, Anne, how does that make you feel?"

How does that make me feel?

How does it make me *f-e-e-l*? Well, confused, enraged, sad, and the same way I have felt every time I've been in a situation with my mother. That's how it makes me feel.

"I guess I wonder why you don't want to read it. But I also wonder something else, Mom. Why didn't you leave a note for us?"

She looks at me sharply. Angry. Then she looks down at the floor. "To be honest, Anne, it never occurred to me."

It's months later that Dr. Levy asks me what I thought of my mother's answer to my question about the suicide note.

"Well, I thought that I have been right all my life about her not being interested in me. What I realized in that moment, though, was that it wasn't just me. She wasn't interested in any of us, or how we might struggle with guilt around our part in her ending her life that way. What we could have done to help her, to see where she was headed."

"Your mother," he says, "like you, mirrors what people want her to be to them, and it made her angry, I think. And the more you start to mirror who you are, and what you want, and invest yourself in the people who you want to be close to, the less anger *you* will have, too."

"I hate it when you compare me to her as if we have any qualities in common or are alike in any way. I hate it."

"You are not your mother. She influenced you, and as you understand how, you can be more and more certain you are not her mirror image."

He has turned out to be right.

DAY SIXTY-EIGHT

I'm walking to meet Eva and Lauren for lunch. This is the first time we will all be together since Lauren's wedding last year. The pretense for the lunch is to discuss the financial situation around Mom's hospitalization and her additional medical expenses, which are now adding up to many tens of thousands of dollars.

I spoke with David and we will pay her expenses, and we will pay for her insurance in the future, but we will not pay for Harvey's. And we will pay her insurance directly. We can do that, and I am happy to make sure she has health insurance in the future, until she goes on Medicare, which is just a few years away.

I'm pretty sure Eva and Lauren expect that will be the plan, so there should be a lot of time to talk about what happened.

I wonder if we will. I wonder how they feel. Angry, like I sometimes am? Sad? I have no idea. I pick up the pace, even though I will be early. I'm excited about the possibility of having lunch together.

They are at the table when I arrive, and while I'm never late, they usually are. I'm glad they cared enough to get here on time.

"Oh my God, I'm so glad to see you both," I say and mean it.

Lauren starts laughing right away. "Have we ever met for lunch, the three of us?"

No, actually, we haven't.

"Let's do it more often," I say.

The waiter arrives and Eva orders wine. Here we go.

We start talking, but not about our mom. We talk about Eva's book. The trip that Lauren and her new husband were on that was cut short. Ali. We talk about a lot of things, and we do it fast. From topic to topic, as if it's a marathon of avoiding silence.

The main course arrives, and I want to get to the point.

"Listen, just want to let you know that David and I will take care of the costs of it all. And Mom's insurance in the future, but not Harvey's. And we will pay it directly, not send them a check to pay it themselves. Done and done."

Silence.

Eva speaks first. "Please thank David for us, okay?"

It strikes me that she isn't thanking me. "Of course."

Lauren says, "Harvey is not going to be okay with that. He's going to say you can't control Mom's insurance."

I don't say anything for a moment and neither does Eva.

"Lauren, I don't know what to say about that. But I will send him an email and he can deal directly with us on it. Does that work? Best to make sure there aren't different people interpreting what everyone is up to. If he doesn't want us to do it, we won't. And, if he does, this is the way we are going to do it."

"Okay, but I'm just saying," and Lauren takes a bite. She looks at me and raises her eyebrows.

I smile back and mean it. "Has anyone talked to Mom about all of this? She keeps saying she wants to speak to us all together, but it's been three months and we haven't done that. Are we going to?"

Eva answers and has a wry grin as she says, "The trouble with you, Anne, is you never learned to read between the lines of the language of our family. Mom will never meet with all of us, and she will never have the conversation she says she wants to have. I was shocked she was willing to go with you to your shrink. Jesus, are you going to tell us what's happening there?"

I pause and realize that she's right. Mom was never ever going to meet with all of us. And, if I don't ask about it, it will never be discussed again.

"You know," I say, "maybe you should ask Mom what's happening in our sessions. I'm grateful she is willing to come, but I can't say that there has been a lightning bolt, Oprah aha moment, or anything."

We all laugh and have coffee and talk about nothing, but it's nice. And I do hope we can do it again. And while I realize that we are not to be trusted, any of us, around each other, I'm grateful that we are connected. And I feel love and happiness to have this time with them.

Eva reaches for the check, and I let her take it. I'm so glad her book is doing well, and I'm so glad she wants to pay for my lunch.

DAY EIGHTY-NINE

We all sit down in his office for the last joint session with my mother and me. I can only assume that Levy will consider this group of sessions his most dismal failure.

My mother opens her bag, takes out an envelope and throws my letter on the table. It's face up and I reach over and turn it over. I'm actually stunned to see that it has not in fact been opened.

"Here is your letter, Anne."

"So, you aren't going to read it?" I ask.

"No."

I stare at the envelope, my name and hers written in my own handwriting. I almost laugh. My letter has become a character in this story, passed around, whispered about, blamed. I pick it up and hold it on my lap. Then I look up and turn to Levy who seems to be without words.

It's the last chapter in my attempt, and maybe hers as well, to try and find a place to connect. I look at Levy and at her, and I have clarity.

"Mom, it's clear that you don't like me. Maybe you never have. It was confusing to me because feeling it and believing it didn't mesh. Everyone would always say, 'Your mother loves you so much. Admires you.' Maybe it would help me, and maybe it would help you, if you could just tell me *why* you never liked me. We'll leave love off the table, but let's start with like." I pause. "Could you do that?"

She looks at me. Levy is looking at me. I look back at her and as God is my witness, I am not going to give her an inch to walk away from the question. I will sit in silence for however long it takes.

Finally, she sits back, looks at me and says, "I don't know why, Anne. I just never have."

And the session is over. And as I leave, the unopened letter is in my pocket.

ONE HOUR LATER

I take the letter to Central Park. I can barely remember what's in it anymore. It's taken on a life of its own, not to be confused with the original intent. The letter has come to be the excuse for it all; the reason no one has had to look at the actions taken, including the woman who took them.

I open it and read it once through and then again out loud.

Dear Mom,

I am writing because we will all be together next week at Eva's book launch, and we haven't spoken since you told me you would call me back in January and never did. You said then that I am just like my father and you can't talk to me. I am not like my father, or like you, or like anyone. I'm me and trying desperately to have a relationship with you based on the two of us. I do so hope that we can. I do so hope that I can be honest in our family. I want to try and be honest with you and have you be honest with me. I don't want to hear through the family grapevine what you think. I do not want to hear things that others in our family can't know. I want to be out of that loop and in one that sings of wishing well for each of us and the accomplishments we all have yet to come, not the failures of yesterday. I love you and I want to know what you think, what you want, what you hope. I hope this letter can serve as the bridge to our new beginning.

Anne

I take the letter and throw it in the trash with the dog poop and the candy wrappers and today's newspapers.

I head home to take Ali to the park, where we are going to swing on the swings and sit in the sun and maybe read a book.

ONE YEAR LATER

A year to the day that my mother tried to kill herself, I'm walking over to meet my sisters for lunch for the second time that year. That's a record. I wonder if they realize that it's a year ago today. I wonder if they measure things the way I do. I wonder if it still affects them, the way it affects me. We haven't seen each other much. After I walked away from the letter in the trash can I was lighter. Emotionally lighter.

I knew that there was no rhyme or reason for this. That I hadn't done anything to make the chasm between my mother and our family the rift that kept us all at a distance. I let it go. I was no longer in therapy. I was often happy. Best to go with lighter. I was lighter.

But I want to have this lunch with my sisters. Aside from wondering if we could have an occasional lunch, the three of us together, enjoying each other, I want the answer to the question that Eva asked me the summer before it all happened. "Please tell our sister to stop trying to kill our mother." It's the only thing that I felt was unresolved.

I arrive at lunch and everybody seems happy to be here. We talk and talk and talk. They tell me things that are going on with Mom and Harvey that I'm clueless about. No surprise there, and I'm able to take it in and laugh at it or feel sad about it but be okay with it. I don't need to fix it. I can't fix it. And even if I could, maybe it was never my issue to fix. And I tell them a bit about what's going on in my world and show them pictures of Ali. It isn't until coffee, two hours later, that I finally bring up what I hope to get some closure on.

"You guys are going to say that I can't just have a good time and have to taint this lunch by bringing up something no one wants to talk about. I own that. But if we're only going to have lunch once a year, can I be allowed one moment where I get to deep sea dive while everybody else water skis? Just one time per lunch?"

They both laugh and we smile and Lauren says, "Sure, go for it. But don't expect us to answer the way you want us to."

I take a moment to pause because I'm sure that what they have to say is something I should remember. I have the expectation that it's not going to serve me the way I want it to. Everybody gets to write their own story and I don't get to write theirs. Okay, okay.

"I promise. I'll do my best. I promise."

Eva says, "What's on your mind?"

"Well, the summer before all this happened, Eva, you told me that Lauren had said, 'Please tell our sister to stop trying to kill our mother.' Okay, in my defense a few months later, Mom tries to kill herself. So, what did you know that I didn't? And on some level, do you guys think it was my fault? And if you do, it's okay. You can tell me. I just want to understand. And no matter what happens in the next few minutes, promise me we're going to have lunch on this very day six months from now. Let's promise."

We all look at each other and smile and promise. And in that moment, we all want it, so if it doesn't happen, it's okay, we had this moment. There's a pause and Eva speaks first.

"We don't need to know things the way you do. We don't need to uncover and put things under a microscope the way that you do. And when you do, and what's under the microscope is often something that's been done to you, it's difficult. And Mom, I think, has always felt that you watched her and judged her in a way that she could never win. And the few months before she tried to kill herself," she pauses, "you were pushing her to try to fix your relationship with her. You don't fix a relationship like that. It's just the way it is. You accept it, try to get what you can out of it, and move on. That's what she wanted you to do, and you couldn't seem to do it. And it made her feel bad."

I sit back and take it all in, and I can understand how they feel. They accepted the terms my mother put on us since birth. I did not. But this new me knows that I'd rather be me than them. That maybe I don't fit into their world, but maybe my world is going to be richer *for me* because of it. I never want to stop asking the questions. But I certainly can see that I'm not my best when I don't get the answers that I need. And that I can do better.

I look at her and say, "Thank you for telling me that. I'm not sure I can be different or even that I want to be. But for sure, if I'm going too deep, then all you have to do is tell me I'm getting into your space, and I will back away. I promise. We're still having lunch in six months, right?"

We all seem relieved and Lauren says, "Well, it depends on where we're going. I didn't like this restaurant and I want to pick it next time."

"Hey, you can pick it every time if you want. I don't care. I just want us to do it."

We walk out of the restaurant arm in arm then head our separate ways, and I think each of us is happy in this moment. That's enough for me.

PART

Two

TWENTY-FIVE YEARS LATER

I sit in the living room of the rental I've been living in on Cape Cod for the past four months. It's the early hours of the morning, and I'm looking out my window at the most magnificent October harvest moon I've ever seen. It's larger than life, right at eye level, and there seems to be a face on it, smiling. The Man in the Moon.

My mother's been gone about three hours. I sit reflecting over the last four months, and I can't possibly fathom the enormity of my mother's life and the things that I didn't know, that I now know. Things that don't make everything okay, but certainly help me understand how she became who she was.

It was four months earlier when she called my office in Los Angeles and told me that she had lung cancer that was spreading and it seemed it was headed to her brain. She asked me to come and take care of things during her last months.

"Mom, I wish this wasn't happening. And I'll come for sure. I'll come right away, but I can't help but wonder why you're calling me instead of my sisters." I started laughing and said, "Mom, you don't even like me."

After that letter moment in time, all those years ago, we had come to a quiet resolution. I stopped trying to fix things between us and she became a little kinder toward me. We saw each other occasionally over the years. And when she was honored in her hometown, I went and sat at her table proudly. And I was happy for her. If I'm to be honest, I didn't think that much about her anymore. My family was my daughter, who was in law school, and I had been divorced for years and had moved to Los Angeles to become vice president of marketing at a large company.

We all were living our lives. I spoke to my sisters occasionally, and saw them at family functions now and then, but basically my nuclear family was the one that I invested in.

She started laughing too, and said, "Anne, if you were dying, who would you call?"

I paused, I think for quite a long time, and then said, "I'll be there on Monday."

Her call came on a Thursday. I drove cross-country to the Cape and told my boss in Los Angeles that I didn't know how long I'd be gone. He said he totally understood and we could do everything by conference call.

The few months went by quickly, filled with family and friends (she was from the Cape), doctor and lawyer appointments, and getting caretakers in, which toward the end was 24/7. It's not that we had intimate conversations and cleared everything up. That's not what happened at all. But there was a peace between us as I took her to her appointments, tried to deal with my sisters, who were constantly second guessing the decisions I was making, and took care of the last-minute things that mattered to her.

My mother was an amazing needle-pointer. She'd been needlepointing for years and had hundreds of pillows and framed needlepoint pieces. She wanted each of them to go to a specific person. She wanted to see people, and she wanted to go to a few places on the Cape where she had moved to spend her last years after Harvey died.

We did all those things, although I still feel guilty because she wanted to go to Provincetown one more time, and I didn't get her there. It was just too much of an effort and I have no excuse. I should have.

I try to remember that I did a lot, or as much as I could. People came from all over to see her and visit and have that one last memory with her, and I saw how many people felt close to her and cared deeply about the loss they would feel when she was gone.

With just a few weeks left, her friend Linda, her best friend for probably forty years, came and stayed with me as there was no room at that point at my mother's place.

Linda doesn't like me. She's from the crowd that I suspect had been told lots of stories about me over the years, and Harvey's testimony that my letter hurt my mother so much she tried to kill herself was one of them.

We are polite to each other, but not much more. She had arrived the day before and spent the day with my mom while I worked. I had stopped over later and we all had dinner, and then Linda came home with me. She is going to stop by and see my mom again in the morning.

As usual, I get up early and make coffee and the two of us are sitting at the kitchen table when it happens.

"Are you going to invite your brother to the funeral?" she asks.

"Linda, I don't have a brother. What are you talking about? I have two sisters. You know that."

She looks at me and she seems to be in a panic.

"Oh, wait, sorry, I don't know what I was thinking. I think this is getting to me. Yeah, no, of course."

I look at her and I know something is not right. It takes me about five seconds to figure out something is going on here.

"Linda, don't say that to me. You didn't make a mistake. What brother are you talking about? Do I have a brother?"

She looks at me and her shoulders drop and then she gets angry, very, very angry.

"Don't be you!" She spits it at me, and spit comes across the table and hits my face. "Just leave it alone. I made a mistake, leave it alone. Your mother's dying. She probably only has a few weeks to live. Just leave it alone. Don't be you."

I look at her and I say, "But Linda, I am me. So, either you tell me what you're talking about or I'm going to go over and ask my mother."

She looks at me and says, "When I saw your mother yesterday, she told me she told you, but it must be the cancer. Yes, you have a brother and he called your mother twenty-five years ago and asked her to see him and she turned him away. She told me she told you." She starts to cry, "Please leave it alone, Anne. Your mother doesn't need this in her last days. Please leave it alone."

I pick up my coffee. I take a sip. "Linda, I hope you have a wonderful time with my mom before you head back to Westport. It was nice to see you. And it meant a lot to my mom that you came all this way to see her. But if my mom told you she told me, maybe she wants me to know. Maybe she wants to see him. I don't know. I have to think about this. Good-bye."

I get up to leave and drive to the beach. I sit thinking about it. I feel that Linda is right; she only has a few weeks left, but what if there is a reason she told Linda she told me. What if she wants to speak to him? To tell him she's sorry. Linda had said he had reached out to my mom. What if she knows his name? What if she doesn't want the secret to be buried with her, all alone in years of grief? And what about my sisters and me? If we have a brother, this might be our last chance to find out who he is.

I drive to my mother's sister's house. My mother and her sister became friends in their later years. They weren't close and didn't speak well of each other until these last years, but somehow, they'd come to a truce, or peace.

I pull into the driveway and sit in the car for a few minutes. I finally get out, knock on the back door, and walk in. My aunt is sitting at the kitchen table drinking coffee. I sit down and my cousin, Michael, who lives with her, comes in and says, "Hey, Cuz, how are you?"

"I'm good, Michael, how are you?"

"Excellent. What are you doing here so early?"

I turn to Sharon and say, "Aunt Sharon, why don't you tell me about my mother's son."

Sharon puts her coffee down on the table.

"How did you find out?"

"Linda told me. She thought my mother had told me, so I'm here to ask you to tell me what happened before I go over to mom's."

The three of us sit there for a long time.

"When your mother was seventeen, she got pregnant. I didn't even know what had happened until years later. Our mother sent her to Philadelphia to have the baby. She gave it up for adoption, and it was never spoken about again. Twenty-five years ago, his wife called your mother and said they had found her and that he wanted to see her. And your mother said no and turned him away. It's been a horrendous time right now because I think your mom regrets that she didn't see him."

I sit back in the chair. I look at Michael, I look at her, and I don't say anything. Twenty-five years. Twenty-five years. Twenty-five years ago was when my mother tried to kill herself. That measuring stick is still in my head; before my mother attempted suicide, after my mother attempted suicide.

I turn to Sharon and say, "Aunt Sharon, is that why my mother tried to kill herself?"

She shrugs her shoulders and says nothing. I let it go.

A few minutes later, I head to my car and call Lauren first.

"Lauren, you're not gonna believe this, but guess what?"

"What," she says, "is Mom okay?"

"Yeah, she's the same. But guess what?"

"I don't know, what?" She's getting irritated and I can't get it out.

"We have a brother."

"Don't be ridiculous. We don't have a brother. What are you talking about?"

"Mom had a baby out of wedlock before she met dad, and gave him up for adoption, and we have a brother." The words rush out and I know I'm not doing it well, and yet here we are.

"What the fuck are you talking about? That can't be true."

"It's true." I tell her the story. I tell her what happened, and her response is, "Leave it alone." And she hangs up on me.

I pull over. I can't believe it. Leave it alone? I sit there and repeat for myself what had happened. The fact that my mother, for some reason, told Linda she had already told me. Didn't that mean she wanted me to know? I sit there wondering if everyone's attacking me about this as if I had anything to do with it, or if maybe they're right. But I realize that I'm running out of time. What if they aren't right?

And if my mom only has a few weeks left, what the fuck difference does it make if she and I have a difficult conversation in a few minutes. She might not even remember it hours from now. But if I don't talk to her, I think it will haunt me. And if this man wanted closure, maybe he deserves one more chance to get it.

I am me, and I am who she wanted to be with these last months of her life. I drive over to her house and Linda's car is gone. I walk in and sit down in her little den area. She is sitting in her easy chair with her feet up and she smiles and says, "Good morning."

"Hi, Mom, how are you doing?"

"I think I'm feeling pretty good today."

"Well, I want to ask you something. You up for it?"

She looks at me, not in a wary way, but I think just curious. And I am looking at her differently, too.

"Mom, Linda told me something when we were having coffee this morning. Did she mention it?"

"No, she just left. She came and said goodbye and I'm glad she came. I'm grateful."

"Mom, she told me that you had a child who was a son before you met Dad. Is that true?"

She looks at me and she breathes what looks to me to be a sigh of relief, but to my sisters, who knows, it might be a sigh of exasperation with having to deal with me.

"Yes, I did."

I try not to fill the void. She smiles at me, and I think I can build the bridge.

"Mom, I don't even know what to say. Do you want to tell me what happened? Do you want me to drop it? Whatever you want, I will do."

"Well, I did. I had a son. May 11, 1949. And they took him." She looks sad, deeply hurt. I pull my chair closer to hers. A few minutes pass and she tells me the story.

She was seventeen, heading off to college in a month or so. She went into a bar and a famous hockey player who had just come back from the Olympics that winter came into the bar, sauntered up to her, and bought her a drink. Then he took her out to the parking lot, saying he would drive her home. In the back of a car, he took her virginity, dropped her off and that was that.

She never says he raped her, but I am struck by who she might have been then, and that she likely didn't have the agency in her to say no. But she never says he forced her.

She went off to college and when she came home for Christmas vacation, her mother knew she was pregnant immediately. She tells me that her mother, who had been the head of nursing at Cape Cod Hospital, had a friend who was a doctor in Philadelphia. The doctor took her in, and for four months she slept on the bench in his patient waiting area, in the office at the front of their home.

She gave birth to a son. They weren't supposed to tell you what the gender was, but a nurse leaned over and said, "It's a boy and he's beautiful and he's perfect. Don't worry." She never held him; she never saw him. She came back from Philadelphia, went to a different college the next fall, and it was never mentioned again.

She tells me that when she was marrying my father, her mother told her she couldn't marry him with such a big lie as a secret; that she would have to tell him what happened, and she did. She says he was the only one who knew, until her son found her years later. And then she told her sister and Linda.

"Aunt Sharon said when he reached out, you turned him away."

That's when the tears start. That's when I see the regret. That's when I see the pain.

"Yes, I did."

"I am so sorry, Mom. Did you not want to meet him? It sounds as if you have had him in your heart all these years. Did you not want to see him?"

"I didn't want to bring the shame upon you girls."

She doesn't say it as if we've done anything wrong. She just says it because it is her truth. Simple, quiet words.

I sit back in my chair. I think about it. I think about the power we all had with her that I didn't even know we had. I think about the years of carrying this around. I think about the twenty-five years after turning him away that must have broken her. I think about her taking the pills that night, and I think about her words when she woke up. "Well, I fucked this up, just like the rest of my life."

I can see that she was broken. She was broken from the time she took that train ride to Philadelphia. She didn't have anything to give us because she had given it all away to a child that she never saw.

And I think it's ironic that my father always wanted a boy and my mother had three girls. I'm sure on some level she must have thought that was her punishment.

I realize in that moment, that we are all who we are because of the things that happen to us, and sometimes because of us. And I'm not saying that it excuses anything or it makes my distance from her all my life better, but I have a little more compassion. I guess I should say I have compassion because before that moment, I don't think I had any.

"Mom, why would you think that we wouldn't have anything but understanding for what you had been through, what so many women have been through? Why would you think that we would think any less of you? Do you think so little of us that we would judge you for what happened when you were seventeen?"

She doesn't say anything. She just looks at me. And I realize that she *had* thought we would have been angry for the upset in our lives. And I realize that she hadn't known any of us at all.

And then it hits me. My younger sister told me to leave it alone. Who knows? Maybe my mother has always known us better than I do. We sit looking at each other with a new bond, a new understanding, maybe. And I forgive her a lot in that moment. I think she knows it.

"Mom, do you want me to try to find him?"

"Yes," she says, "I do. I want to see him."

"Do you remember his name?"

She spells it out. "His name is Timothy Haidler, H-a-i-d-l-e-r. He lives in Norwalk." Norwalk? Ten minutes from Westport? Wow. I get my iPad. I type in the name, grateful that it is an unusual one. And I type in Norwalk and there he is. Tim Haidler, and he owns a restaurant. I get a phone number, and then I see pictures of him and I stop short. He is my mirror image.

I call the number and it is his son's wife who answers. She immediately knows exactly what I'm talking about and says, "Please give me your phone number right now and I'll make sure he calls you right back. This will mean so much to him. Please answer the phone."

I tell her I will, and I go sit in the car to wait. Fifteen minutes later the phone rings.

"Hello," I say.

"Hi, Sis. It's your brother, Tim."

We talk for two hours. He tells me that he had contacted my mother and had understood why she didn't want to blow up her family and her position in the community. But living in the town next door, he had followed her political career, and that he knows a bit about us as well.

So, there was this family who knew about us, who kept my mother's secret because she wanted him to, and who gave up so much to do it because this moment meant so much to him. And I am grateful.

I ask him if he can come and I tell him she doesn't have much longer.

He says, "I'll be there tomorrow."

I sit for a moment before going in to tell my mom he will come to see her the next day. I think about the enormity of the secret she has kept all these years. How it defined her. It has also defined our relationship, but without me having the knowledge to put it in perspective. This day has taken all that was out of focus from our history and has brought a clarity I will need time to decipher.

She and I sit for a while, and she tells me more stories about how the years have been with him in her thoughts, but no one else's. He was always in the room, but no one else saw him. How on Christmas, she always bought a present for him and then gave it to someone else. At Thanksgiving, she had wondered what the table would have been like with him at it.

How when she watched Oprah find out that she had a sister that had been a secret, she had wondered if maybe she could tell us. But had soon realized it was too late. Too many lies would be uncovered. She would no longer be who she was to us all. It had seemed to her that it was always too late.

"All these years, and now, when I have no time left, it's out and I can't help but think how these last years could have been so different."

And the words do not have one inch of "poor me." More of a wonder at what could have been.

I don't tell her that he has three children, and she has three more grandchildren, school age. I don't tell her how he'd been a world champion powerboat racer. That I had already watched the YouTube video where he humbly did an interview, and the reporter had introduced him as the most liked racer on the circuit.

I don't tell her that he has dimples just like mine, and that he is shy on camera the way she is.

She tells me that she thought she saw him in a parade, years and years ago, marching with the Cub Scouts. It turns out he did march in that parade, and I think about how she was on the side of the street and saw a boy she had never seen in a sea of other boys, with three young girls at her side, and it was him.

And, how I now know that over the years she must have looked at every boy's face that was his age at the time, to see if maybe it was him. For years.

She tells me she went to his restaurant after he called and sat in the parking lot. That she had watched him leave and cried.

We have a quiet dinner, just the two of us. I hug her when I leave to head home. She just sits there, but it's okay. It's my message to her that I can't comprehend her life, but I had heard her.

When I get home, I light a candle and go outside and sit as the sun is setting, thinking about everything. My own hubris is my first stop. How it never occurred to me that my mother had secrets that she couldn't share, not because she was afraid of anybody's response, but because they were so bad. Her sin was so unforgiveable that she couldn't come back from it. There was no new year anticipation for what could change in the next.

She walked away from her child. Twice. I want to tell her that she was seventeen years old in 1949, headed to college, with a formidable mother, and totally dependent on her parents and the pattern of saying "yes" when they told her to. It was ingrained in her responses. Part of her DNA. And back then, she would not have had the option to go it alone. Not from the world she had grown up in.

She didn't have the agency that my own experience provided. My heart ached for her, but also for me. That our DNA pattern of not getting into the mess of personal pain was so deep, so ingrained, that I didn't feel like I could give her the comfort she deserved, or that she would even want me to.

I knew that I was always trying to tell myself and others that I wasn't my mother, but the need to do that was based on my lack of understanding that her road made her who she was, and mine made me who I am. And while we had crossed paths, intersected, we had never journeyed together toward a common destination.

There was too big a secret stopping her from going anywhere outside her own world. So deep and dark and so filled with shame that it meant my mother didn't want to be my mother. Or anyone's mother.

I quietly cry, realizing how hard I had been on her when she was probably spending most of her days being hard on herself.

And the lack of joy was not because of anything other than this one thing that she had done in her life that was so terrible, so awful, so dirty, that she never forgave herself or moved on. And that she would never really see it for what it was. The wrong place, on the wrong night, with the wrong guy, that changed her life forever.

I've had things I'm sorry for having done to others. I've learned to apologize and move on. They still show up, but they do not stop me from ever moving forward from that moment. I am luckier than my mom.

As I'm blowing out the candle and heading to bed, I think about his visit tomorrow. How the opportunity for closure, or some sort of something, is possible for them both. And, then I sleep the deep sleep from which dreams are made, but usually not remembered.

He comes to see my mother the next morning and I leave them to get pizza to bring back a few hours later. I have no idea what's been said between them. But before he leaves, my mother gives him some needlepoint pillows, and I think she does it because that's all she has to give him. And she is so sad when he leaves.

She weeps and I wish I could tell you that I put my arms around her, but I didn't. I just sat there patting her, wishing I was closer, but knowing that that ship had sailed years ago.

He comes to see her one more time before she passes away, and I tell him I want him to sit with us at her funeral, and I hope he will get some peace around what happened to him.

So, as I sit here, I know I have to tell my sisters tomorrow that he and his wife will be with us at the funeral, and I will deal with that if it's a problem then.

There's another secret. I know who his father is, and my mother is right, he's a famous man in sports. She had told me she doesn't want Tim to know, but I'm not sure I will keep her secret now that she's gone. I have to decide if it's part of the past and should be left there, or if it's just me perpetuating the toxicity of lies and secrets that build up in a family like ours. I don't know yet.

I look at the moon again, at this harvest moon that has this huge face on it. And I think about the conversation my mother and I had a month earlier. The radiation on her brain had blown her face up, and I laughingly told her one day, "You look like the Man in the Moon, Mom. It's a good look for you."

A few days later, we were talking about whether there was a life after death, which was nothing our family had ever spent any time considering.

"Mom, if there is, show me a sign, some kind of sign if you can, okay?"

"I will do it. I promise."

And literally an hour after she passed away, just two hours ago, I had walked out her front door after they removed her from the house, and there was the man's face on the moon. I now believe you can believe whatever you want, you can look at a "sign" and think it means something, or not.

I lie down on the couch with the thought that the moon will now hold a special connection to my mom in death that I never had when she was alive. As I drift off to sleep, I realize that I've spent a lifetime trying to prove to myself that I'm not my mother. It had never occurred to me that while that is true, perhaps more importantly, my mom was not me. She never had the chance with the burden she carried.

I'm sorry I didn't recognize that earlier. As I look out at the moon, though, I have a feeling she knows that now, too.

EPILOGUE

From my blog a month after my mom died...

November 11

My mom died. I haven't written my blog in a while because she is gone, and I just don't know how to make things seem normal when they are not. How can I possibly write as if nothing has changed when everything has changed forever? I recognize that everyone's mother dies. I think they call it the Cycle of Life, and I used to offer that phrase to others as a consolation. But now it seems superficial and irritating. I will never say it again.

For me, the fact that the sun came out the very next day, that my cell phone continued to ring with business calls from people seeking answers to questions they had asked the day before, is unthinkable. The fact that I laughed not forty-eight hours after my mom stopped breathing seems criminal.

You see, I was not finished with her. I have not asked her all I need to know. I was just learning things about her that seemed to make sense of other things. I didn't get to take her on that last trip she wanted to make to Provincetown. I forgot to ask her where she wanted all those needlepoint pillows to go. I wasn't finished, and neither was she.

I didn't want to write about her here. Way too public. But the thing is, if I don't write about her here, I can't write about anything else. For if my mom deserved nothing more, she deserved to have something stop for a while to mark the moment when she left us. And so that marker will be this post to her. It's the only thing I have that I can stop for a time to lay her to rest properly. Nothing else has a stop button.

Let me introduce the best of my mother to you here. The rest of her will go somewhere on the cobwebbed shelves of my mind, where it will haunt me now and then, but will never again see the light of day. I get to do that now. I get to rewrite the future of our relationship as what I always wanted it to be, so I can bring her with me for a moment during an evening and not have to worry about getting her home. I can bring her to that part of the movie that she would have liked. I can ask her to send me a sign, and I can see that sign if I want to. Everything about the two of us will now be exactly as I want it, and that should be something, right?

My mom was quieter than me in every way. We had very different political views. I realized as I was struggling to write her eulogy that she never once tried to change my political leanings, while I tried relentlessly to change hers. She accepted things that I would never have accepted. She accepted other people, including me, the way they were, without trying to make them into something they were not meant to be, or didn't want to be. I like that about her now.

I like that she would give you anything you wanted; she had no real investment in her things. My late mother-in-law, who was my beloved mentor, once told me that within a few days of her death all that she had acquired over the course of nearly 100 years would be dispersed as if no one had ever gathered it.

She was right. My mother, on the other hand, gave away much of what she had, so that scattering of belongings will not be so dramatic as I go through them. Her things live in homes all over the place. Her friends, family, my friends, and strangers have had her things with them since long before she left us.

My mom was the mother who waited for you to call her, just in case a call from her would bother you. She didn't brag about her own achievements, only those of others. Her sense of humor sometimes involved sleight of hand, and was occasionally for her benefit alone. This summer I gave her an Obama mug, just to drive her crazy. I told her there were only 1,000 of them that he was giving away. She asked me if I could get ten more of them. I was pleasantly shocked and got them, which was not easy, I might add. The next day I went into her kitchen and saw that she had put them in the garbage. When I indignantly asked her why, she replied, "You said they were a limited edition. I figured that would be ten more that no one would get to see." It was her joke to herself. She would never have told me she did that. I would have needed to tell people. She never did. In her honor I have vowed to play one joke, once a year, that is for me alone. Just her and me.

That's it. Nothing more. The sun is still shining into my office. Nothing has changed since I started writing this, and tomorrow I will be back to my blog as you have known it. But for the last three weeks it stopped to mark the passing of my mom, Mary Ann Ilse, who lived for eighty-two years the very best she could.

ACKNOWLEDGEMENTS

To my editor, my friend, and collaborator, Carol Rea, who makes sure I do my best work—no matter how long it takes. I'm especially grateful for her understanding and appreciation of my voice, even when it doesn't always align with the Grammar Queen she is at heart. Every time I sit down to write, I'm thankful knowing she's there, watching, making sure I get it right.

Book number two, Carlotta!

ABOUT THE AUTHOR

Christine Merser is a marketing strategist, successful writer, and entrepreneur whose literary work spans both fiction and nonfiction. She is the author of *Flight of the Starling*, the first book in her trilogy exploring a woman's foray into black ops after her billionaire friend asks her to go to the Middle East to rescue his trafficked daughter, with the second installment set to launch in late 2025.

Her political blog, *America Interrupted Dispatch*, can be found on Substack, where she chronicles the complexities of today's political landscape. She also shares personal reflections through her memoir writing, which has been published in numerous magazines over the past two decades.

Christine is a passionate advocate for film and television as a medium for social change, particularly from a female perspective. As a film reviewer and podcast host for *Her Screen Thoughts*, she believes in the power of storytelling: "For me, film and television have always been a way to change hearts and minds without anger or discord."

Beyond her writing, Christine is a thought collaborator around women's roles in business. Her new book, *Circles of Collaboration*, explores a business philosophy rooted in the history of women's success through collaborative circles, where everyone brings their expertise in equal measure.

The Letter is a deeply personal story about a mother's suicide attempt and the unraveling of their relationship—an experience that ultimately leads to liberation from the impossible expectation of being the daughter her mother would have loved.

\